PECKINPAH SUITE

By the same author:

Books:

Henderskelfe (with photographs of Castle Howard by Peter Heaton)
Asterisk (with photographs of Shandy Hall by Marion Frith)
Analogue/Digital: New & Selected Poems
The Bulmer Murder
Chromatic
Amplitude
Unclassified: Nigel Kennedy in Chapters and Verse

Chapbooks:

Keys; Fire; Orange; Rhyme; Sound; The Music Lovers; Iron Age; Sweet; Pacific; Poems of 2024–25

As editor:

Reading the Applause (with Stephen Wade)
Feeling the Pressure: Poetry and science of climate change
Strange Cargo: Five Australian Poets
Tract: Prose poems (with Monica Carroll)
Metamorphic: 21st century poets respond to Ovid (with Nessa O'Mahony)
Abstractions (with Shane Strange)
Giant Steps (with Shane Strange)
No News (with Shane Strange and Alvin Pang)
Divining Dante (with Nessa O'Mahony)

Screenplay:

The Darkroom (with Kit Monkman, Thomas Mattinson, Hettie Shirazu)

PECKINPAH SUITE

PAUL MUNDEN

RECENT WORK PRESS
2015-2025
10 YEARS OF POETRY

Peckinpah Suite
Recent Work Press
Canberra, Australia

Copyright © Paul Munden, 2025

ISBN: 9781763670167 (paperback)

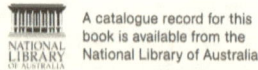
A catalogue record for this book is available from the National Library of Australia

All rights reserved. This book is copyright. Except for private study, research, criticism or reviews as permitted under the Copyright Act, no part of this book may be reproduced, stored in a retrieval system, or transmitted in any form by any means without prior written permission. Enquiries should be addressed to the publisher.

Cover image: door to the Peckinpah Suite in the Murray Hotel, Livingston, Montana. Photograph by Zoe Randall, adapted by Oswin Wan.
Set by Recent Work Press

recentworkpress.com
10 YEARS OF POETRY

'All I want is to enter my house justified.'
—Steve Judd in *Ride the High Country*

Contents

PRELUDE

Room 322 — 2

PART I

Red and Green	6
Gunsmoke	8
Reading, Writing	10
The Westerner	12
Brown	14
The Deadly Companions	16
Ride the High Country	18
The Losers	20
Major Dundee	22
The Cincinnati Kid	24
Noon Wine	26
The Wild Bunch	28
Kansas City, 1 May 1969	30
The Lizard Lounge	32
The Ballad of Cable Hogue	34
Play It As It Lays	36
Straw Dogs	38
Junior Bonner	40
The Getaway	42
Pat Garrett and Billy the Kid	44
Knives	46
Bring Me the Head of Alfredo Garcia	48
The Killer Elite	50
Soldiers Three	52
Cross of Iron	54
Post-production	56
Convoy	58
Montana, 1978	60
Cabin Fever	62

PART II

Castaway   65

PART III

The Emergency Room   80
Montana, 1979   82
Latigo Productions   84
The Osterman Weekend   86
Too Late for Goodbyes   88
On the Rocks   90
The Ones That Got Away   92
Begonia   94
Solomon's Island   96
Paradise Cove   98
Sunset Boulevard   100

CODA

The Racquet Club   104

PRELUDE

Room 322

I pause at the entrance
to this strange suite
of rooms, once yours.
Anyone can check in here
for 649 dollars a night.
I ask myself *why*,
even as I pull a credit

> card from my wallet,
> wondering if this
> might yet be the space
> where a masterpiece
> gets written—written
> or possibly forgotten
> as things un-

ravel in a coke-
crazed haze, and all
those we claim to love
take a battering worse
than the old Remington
still suffers—or enjoys.
The original wooden door

is riddled with bullet
holes, though I realize
that's just in my mind's eye
where there's also a sign—
THE OLD IGUANA
SLEEPS AND THE ANSWER
IS NO—hanging askew.

I ignore it, hear you hiss
at the intrusion.
Hard to tell if the force
with which I seem to feel
you hit the expectant keys
is passionate with right
or wrong; if what

>   abides here will prove
>   to be an inspiration
>   or mere curse;
>   something to entrance
>   or simply appal.
>   I hang the sign anew
>   and get to work.

PART I

Red and Green

You were cleaning the innards
from fish you had caught
with your grandfather
when your knife
slipped, slicing an artery.
You watched, thrilled
by the bright red blood

>pumping from your arm,
>like Sylvia Plath, numb
>to the pain in her thumb
>when she cut it instead
>of an onion.
>*The blood jet is poetry.*
>Grandpa Denver Church

was quick to patch
you up while you still
silently marvelled
at what you had seen,
the hidden pulse of life
made visible, the near
calamity like a charm.

Years later, at Broad Beach,
charm was alive and well
when Walter Peter fell
backwards out
of a first floor
window, and in
the blink of an eye

reappeared
at your front door.
That was the start of it:
The Nation of Green,
a crazy brother-
hood of self-rule, a parallel
world so exclusive that

       someone had to die
       before anyone
       else could be enrolled.
       Green: a land where
       fantasy and sheer
       bloody-mindedness held
       all the cards.

Gunsmoke

We forget, perhaps,
what being dead was like
when we played cowboys
in the woods, counting
from one to a hundred
with a mounting
visceral dread

> that the bad guys—
> by which I mean everyone—
> had moved on. But since
> our lives were mostly play
> back then, death—
> by which I mean our pretence—
> was how we got from day

to day, holding our breath
for as long as it took
to sense the danger.
We watched *The Lone Ranger*.
We wanted the big white hat,
the mask, and that
crucial accessory, the gun.

For a while we made do
with our own two
tightly barrelled fingers,
waited until birthdays
or Christmas
for the gun itself, complete
with a paper reel

of powder-charged caps
from which came what
we'd never known
onscreen—a sulphurous
smell, curling with the smoke
from the gun's report
to where it still lingers.

From then on, I smelt it
in every cinematic bullet,
a miracle I'd soon yearn
to recreate,
if not as the man
behind the camera, then
with my own best skill.

Reading, Writing

The way you'd happily lose
yourself in a book
reminds me how I once
found my daughter kneeling
precariously on the edge
of the kitchen table,
head down in heaven

      knows what. Same age,
      you're reading *Castaway*,
      the story you would
      return to all your life,
      so engrossed you don't hear
      your grandfather approach
      to clip you round the ear

and kick you outside
into the fresh air.
You're not that much
older when he goes further,
throwing you a rifle,
his plan then to despatch
you with your brother

       into the High Sierras
       hunting for deer.
       You know the awful
       truth: a kill means food
       but still—from your vantage
       point on the bluff—
       you're unable

to pull the trigger without
remorse. Not a day
goes by without the look
in the animal's eye stealing
up on you unaware.
And try as you may
to muster some pretence

              at being forgiven,
              you'll never evade
              the brutal charge;
              can't forget
              the slow spread of blood
              in the snow, or the need
              to tell us how it was.

The Westerner

Still learning your trade,
you're granted a luxury
you'll never have again,
producing a whole series
of your own—thirteen
episodes in which to test
the limits of the form.

> Here, for the first time,
> you make your point
> about a gunshot wound,
> not yet with lurid blood
> that spurts into the air,
> but showing us the scar
> on a man where a bullet

once entered—and
its grossly magnified twin
where flesh burst loose
on the other side.
Until now, a TV western
had been prime-time fare
for kids. No *pain*.

The eponymous lead,
Dave Blassingame,
is partly to blame
for everything that occurs,
though his genial calm
is also the blessing bestowed
on every showdown.

It's a vicious moral maze
of betrayals, but beneath
every brawl there's some
emotional injury,
a romantic obsession
unfulfilled. You cast
your own wife as a haggard

       evangelical, poised in front
       of the graffiti you want
       us to contemplate
       like a confession:
       Tonight a soul is lost.
       He wanders the wide earth
       but he finds only emptiness.

Brown

How the hell did you coax
and capture a performance
of such comic virtuosity
from a *dog*, 'Brown',
chasing a gang of cats
into a general store
and demolishing the place?

      Brown, companionable
      as a bottle of the same,
      and as fickle—
      he may slurp beer
      with his master at the bar,
      but he's not fussed who
      that master might be.

Dave Blassingame
will likewise disown him
to get out of a fix,
or, in frequent despair,
mock his stupidity.
When Dave is bound
with rope and has to call

            his four-legged friend
            to the rescue, we
            gasp as the idiot hound
            jumps right through
            a shattering glass
            window, but then gets
            side-tracked by food

left on the table.
And yet the two of them
are inseparable.
We know for sure
that Dave has been sun–
struck by gold when
he won't share

            so much as a trickle
            of water, or glance
            back to the poor animal
            who'll prove to be his own
            better self, his conscience,
            refusing to continue
            along a path to no good.

The Deadly Companions

The pattern is set: trouble
from the start—no scope
to refine a problematic script.
Brian Keith is on your side
but you're not even allowed
to talk to his co-star,
Maureen O'Hara,

> who considers you inept,
> strange, objectionable.
> Faced with her cabal
> you have no real control,
> but many images still work
> as intriguing pre-echoes
> of themes you'll develop

in films to come: kids
play-fighting in the street;
that harmonica; and a corpse
as disquieting companion
to the misfits
trekking through the desert.
On their trail

      is a lone Apache Indian
      who, in a lightning-struck
      close-up, stares
      down across
      the vertiginous dark
      into the heart
      of our primitive fears.

You'll eventually joke
that it could have played
as comedy—a few buzzards
perhaps, circling overhead
as the stench of the dead
child became too plausible
to ignore. As it is,

      you have to conclude
      with a scene that defies
      any logic or excuse:
      actors passing like ships
      in the all too day-bright night;
      no-one able to decide
      who finally calls the shots.

Ride the High Country

Mountain-clear water
framed by gold foliage—
your childhood landscape
where you'd one day return
to build a wilderness lodge.
The soft autumnal hues
border on nostalgia,

> even for me, a stranger
> here in the Old West.
> Coarsegold was higher up
> and needed to look it,
> but the wrong weather
> on the tightest budget
> made you improvise

with scattered soap-
flakes to capture the chill.
Gold, friendship, betrayal…
but hidden within this tale
is the fact of a father
and daughter who'll
never see each other again.

I'm increasingly lost
in my trivial quest
for Dinkey Creek—
watching the mileage
clock up as the trail
goes cold—all because
of my little one's pet name.

As we near the end,
a scene of unnatural calm
is broken by a quick
ground-level zoom
to the father not at prayer
but propped there
dead: it's a trap.

> They used an altogether
> different title in England:
> *Guns in the Afternoon.*
> Neither seems right to me,
> for whom it will always be
> *The Only One
> I Watched With My Daughter.*

The Losers

Once upon a time
nerves made you vomit
before going on set.
Now you've the stomach
for getting the job done
unperturbed, though still
full of free spirit

>   like a kid in a sandpit.
>   You pick up Blassingame
>   and Burgundy Smith
>   like figures from folklore,
>   rascals who can drift
>   from one wild west town
>   to the next, one era

to another. You drop them
into a Texan city hotel
as card sharps, soon
running pell-mell
from their marks,
your camera
caught up in the quick/

      slow, forward/back
      madcap fun—
      and so the game goes on.
      Within the span
      of a frantic fifty-minute
      picaresque, you let
      your hapless duo roam

into multiple misfit
worlds, lives—a random
family in the making—with
Brown of course in tow
(almost stealing the show).
Beguiled, we follow
each unexpected shift

      of mood as you fill
      the small screen
      with silver-tongued wit
      and big-screen sparks,
      a promise of what more
      might be to come—
      if only the losers would win.

Major Dundee

Massacred. *Butchered*—
the uncompromising word
for the families' fate
when the Apache horde
desecrates their homestead
at Halloween; also for how
your cherished picture

> was torn apart
> as the studio cut what
> the story was all about.
> We'll never see the almost
> subliminal images you shot
> of the children dressed
> up as those Indians,

spliced into the raid.
Amos Dundee is Ahab
on a horseback quest
for his own dark soul.
And even as you fall out
with Heston in the role,
so that he threatens

you with his sword,
you're siding with his rage,
sacrificing narrative structure
in the name of your fight
with the producers—a mob
now baying for your blood.
Laziness in the savage

Columbia edit
leaves in the briefest
glimpse of the slow-
motion carnage
they simply didn't get.
Having done their worst—
your concept fully defiled—

    the opening credits roll
    to the upbeat, martial tones
    of the Mitch Miller Sing
    Along Gang.
    Your anger and hurt
    know no limit.
    It's like losing a child.

The Cincinnati Kid

Black and white it would be:
months of verbal combat
resolved, it would seem,
in your favour—the grit
of those depression years
and the poker-faced souls
who thrived within it.

> You take your time to strip
> the carefully cluttered set
> back to a few details.
> A dark-skinned whore
> lets the fur coat slip
> from her naked shoulders:
> you film the scene

from every angle to ensure
you have the shot you need
to define the woman's sad
complicity—the whole
heart of the story—in vain.
Your meticulous quest
is also the cause

>   of your demise,
>   proof of your bad attitude.
>   They want popcorn fare,
>   soft Butch Cassidy, not
>   the real Bunch. Aware
>   of your enemies,
>   you flush them out ...

You won the battle and lost
the war, almost before
it had begun. Who knows
what otherwise
might have been—
the surge of acclaim
and a lifelong stream

>   of bankable offers. Instead,
>   violence became your
>   reactionary theme.
>   They wanted you gone.
>   You wanted your full fee
>   and got exile into the bargain.
>   They got their colour after all.

Noon Wine

Producer Daniel Melnick
has put his own neck
on the line to put you back
behind a camera: Never mind
that it's just TV: you're not
gonna blow it—fan of the book
by Katherine Anne Porter.

> You're given proper time
> to rehearse a top-notch cast:
> Robards, de Havilland,
> and Theodore Bikel
> as the laughing hyena
> of a bounty hunter,
> Homer T Hatch.

Per Oscarsson as Helton
is the disturbing stranger
in an even stranger land
where trust and deceit
are somehow complicit
in how tragedy grows
from one violent spark.

You use the geometry
of the smaller screen
to perfection, even while
broadening its horizon—
the disintegrating years
of a marriage, all within
an hour. The high-angle shot

of Robards' slow walk from
the house, top right corner,
across the yard at night—
flashlight and shotgun in hand—
to the barn where he'll write
his suicide note,
bottom left, is visual poetry

      at its simplest and best.
      The show gets rave reviews
      but your biographical touch
      comes at a cost:
      for your mother it's much
      too close to home,
      to the bone.

The Wild Bunch

Three wilderness years
have made you plan
this believing your life
depends on it, but
still you're up at sunrise
staring into space as if
conjuring a miracle.

    The hacienda courtyard
    is empty as you search
    its unnerving terrain
    for how the Bloody Porch
    battle will play out.
    Just managing the squib-
    blown wardrobe

will be a military campaign.
Six cameras are to run
at different speeds,
each actor six-times dead
as you laboriously shift
angles across the body-strewn
ground, five slow feet

at a time. You've rebuilt
an original 1910 steam
locomotive from scratch,
acquired dynamite galore
from the Mexican army.
But for every whore
who tends to your needs

by night, there's an inept
hired hand, an enemy
within, to be sent home
the next day. You've only one
shot at this—lighting the fuse
that must splinter the bridge
into a panoramic spectacle

of havoc. Nothing can be left
to chance, and yet—
for all this absolute
precision—right now none
of these legendary, lyrical
sequences exist, except
in your own visionary head.

Kansas City, 1 May 1969

The first preview
is a riot—a thousand mid-
westerners expecting
a good ol' fashioned
horse opera stunned
by the onslaught
of images on screen.

> But for every person
> traumatized
> by what they see,
> another is mesmerized
> by the almost erotic ballet
> of bad men in the throes
> of death; bad, but not

beyond redemption. Those
outraged want blood,
with no apparent sense
of irony. Do you
stand your moral ground,
or run? You're a rabbit
in the headlights of fame.

William Holden's line—
If they move, kill 'em—
will soon become
the frequent caption
to the simplistic *Bloody Sam*,
censorious shorthand
for the floodgates opened

to excess—never mind
that the sickening Mỹ Lai
massacre had already outdone
anything you might dream.
Questioned, your response
is rid of all pretence,
but full of the greater crime—

>   *explanation.*
>   I try to imagine
>   being there, in the audience,
>   incredulous, unprepared.
>   Here's a reaction card,
>   blank, as if still waiting
>   for my timely opinion.

The Lizard Lounge

You film *Ballad* back
to back with *The Bunch*.
It's supposed to be a breeze—
this story of how Cable
stumbles on a water-hole
and his future. But it's you
that finds water where

>it's almost unknown:
>more rain in fifteen days
>than in the thirty years
>before. Everyone gets ill—
>Slim Pickens nearly dies
>of pneumonia. Fable
>is re-written in the bar

of The Echo Bay Hotel
with your stock company
behaving true to form.
Practical jokes
escalate; one punch
leads to a brawl, while
Warner recites Shakespeare

and Gillis plays guitar.
Your temper is short.
Anyone who provokes
you will have rattlesnakes
thrown into the pit
of their own making, or
be dismissed—so many

fired, the bus back to town
works overtime. When
you lose a poker game
you shred a pile of dollar
bills and throw the lot
to the coyotes that prowl
outside. The barman,

who's grown fond
of you and all your crew,
is preparing a bill
nearing a hundred grand.
The coyotes howl.
You give one of them a collar
and a role in the film.

The Ballad of Cable Hogue

This is as close as you'll get
to showing us love
between a man
and a woman—a whore
who's *the ladiest damn'd lady*;
Cable the charming illiterate
willing to blow his grub-

       stake on a night with her,
       the face on a dollar bill
       twinkling into the smile
       that leads him on.
       Where the Bloody Porch
       agony was drawn out,
       here the gentle comedy

is speeded up
into frenetic slapstick:
the slimeball Reverend
Joshua Duncan Sloan
scampering from his mis-
judged misdemeanours;
Cable flapping with a sheet

      to cover Hildy's naked body
      as she jumps from the tub
      when the stagecoach
      takes them by surprise.
      You take your time,
      though, in helping them
      agree to leave

for new horizons. A car—
what the devil?—is at hand
to drive them from the desert
when poor Cable has to trip
the brake and fall
under its wheels. Still
he manages to joke

           about the eulogy he might
           be given, but the fairytale
           darkens before our eyes,
           the faux tribute
           suddenly a real funeral,
           night now closing in
           on his dust-blown cathedral.

Play It As It Lays

I'm reading Didion's book
and imagining it
as the film she so
wanted you to make—
she and her husband
John Gregory Dunne,
but no-one else

      in the business,
      no-one in this Hollywood
      stripped of its glamour
      by the scalpel of her prose.
      They could only suppose
      that you, the outcast, would
      twist the knife even

deeper, with a sense
of personal grievance.
And what had you ever done
but westerns? Why trust
you with this portrait
of a marriage gone bad?
I think instead: *why not*.

You know all too well
of domestic violence,
There's hardly a gun
in sight, but there's blood
in abundance—
a woman's blood, shed
for an insidious truce

that leaves her destroyed
but still resisting suicide.
Her four-year-old girl
is already collateral
damage, smashing her doll
into a mirror,
the very image of lost

>innocence.
>*Why not*, the woman
>declares at the end,
>in terrible acceptance
>of her lot, an echo
>of your own famous line.
>If only a studio had agreed.

Straw Dogs

We sneaked off school
to watch it at the Gaumont,
my visceral fear a match
for my astonishment
at how the story
was put together
with the same cool

        precision with which
        timid Mr Sumner does
        his blackboard sums –
        then transforms
        into methodical demon,
        so that every gory
        consequence

made terrifying sense.
Later, it was shown
at school anyway. We were
warned to leave the room
if it was all too much,
but we remained,
as have images, engrained

        forever on the mind.
        Is that me?—I'm asked
        of Dustin Hoffman
        raising a glass of scotch
        with (it seems) my wife,
        framed on my wall.
        And there you are

below, in black and white,
with that clown of a rat-
catcher, mucking about
at Trencher's Farm
on the same tricycle
I rode in an endless circle
around the small lawn

        of my childhood home,
        my mother or father
        catching me on film.
        There never was
        any real licence
        to escape: I've tasked
        myself with the proof.

Junior Bonner

Seen one rodeo, seen 'em all
comes the dull dismissal
at the Bonner family meal
on the eve of the real-
time annual Prescott
event for which you place
a camera on every rooftop

    to focus right in
    on your personal story.
    Its reception will be tough:
    one day you'll joke
    that you *made a film*
    where nobody got shot
    and nobody went to see it.

It's man against animal,
man against machine
and, briefly—when a black
bull breaks from the chute
and through the fourth wall,
smashing a pricey camera—
beast against budget.

Joe Don Baker, in the role
of the brother who destroys
the family home
to make a trailer park,
thinks you're a prick,
but the noise of his bull-
dozers grinds deep

into your memory—
your mother selling off
your grandfather's ranch.
So when JR punches him
to the floor you shake
your head: the punch
must be repeated, take

after take. Blink, and we miss
you onscreen as an extra
in the crowded Palace Bar,
making sure all
drinks are on the house
and the brawl that ensues
is authentic chaos.

The Getaway

In a Texas prison, the noise
of workshop machines
is relentless, as Doc McCoy
in his cell, a matchstick
model bridge in his hands,
suddenly crushes it.
Outside there are deer

> quietly grazing; wardens
> posturing as cowboys.
> Doc is a bad man
> in a world that's worse—
> his own wife duplicitous
> in his conditional release
> to work with double-

dealing scum on a heist.
But he's Steve McQueen
so we assume the best—
until, that is, we witness
him slap his wife's face
by a deserted highway
where a sign—MUNDENS—

       casts me as accomplice.
       Here, in these heartlands
       of redneck America,
       Doc can just buy
       a pump-action shotgun
       over the counter and blast
       his way out of trouble.

There was a subtle score
for all this—discreet
as *a man in a green suit*
walking in a forest—
which McQueen replaced
with ruthless harmonica.
A grinding garbage truck

       dumps the McCoys
       like trash that might yet
       find fugitive grace.
       And there you are, your back
       to us, on the sidewalk,
       arm around your latest
       amour, waiting to cross.

Pat Garrett and Billy the Kid

A man who has nothing to do
with the narrative
drifts slowly downstream
on a ramshackle houseboat
in the half-light of dawn,
takes aim at a bottle afloat
ahead of him in the water

       and misses. *No way,*
       say the producers, their eye
       on schedule and budget—
       the imperative
       of all-out thrills, not
       The story of a man who
       doesn't want to run

being chased by a man
who doesn't want to catch him.
So you order your crew
to steal away, film it in secret—
this beautiful, wild west
poem in which Garrett,
on the riverbank, is drawn

       into the mindless target
       practice and face-
       off with the stranger. Later
       he will shoot first
       his own former friend,
       Billy the Kid,
       then his own image

in a mirror, a scene
you've rehearsed
forever in your head.
You have a cameo
as the weary carpenter
preparing to bury the legend
itself. When the studio

       takes all this footage
       away from you
       it's both a sad crime
       and fractured dream.
       We do our best to piece
       together every last
       sliver of silvered glass.

Knives

I whittled away hours
at my solitary pursuit,
my mother's wireless
a soft accompaniment
from the kitchen window
behind me, as I drew
my latest purchase

> from its leather sheath,
> feeling a greater weight
> when I took the blade
> between my fingers, and—
> with a flick of the wrist—
> released it to spin
> and plant itself blade first

into the earth.
At least, that was the plan.
In practising my art
I too often made a hash
of it, misjudging the distance
so that the handle instead
would thud

against the ground.
It's hard to believe
you would choose
to do this from your bed—
hurling the knife
towards the scarred door
where at any moment

someone might walk in.
Fearing the worst
makes me see it in slow-
motion, the knife leave-
ing your hand, twist-
ing its way through the air
as the door

opens and a friend
stands framed, her life
in the balance.
And why would I share
this—my intensifying fear
of what never then occurred—
unless I'm similarly rash?

Bring Me the Head of Alfredo Garcia

Outlawed from Hollywood
again, you're free to make
the film you want, master-
piece or disaster
(the jury's still out);
either way, the mayhem's
all on your own terms.

       I have to bend my pro-
       noun rules, as Warren Oates
       is half *you* in his portrayal
       of the ruthless romantic
       saddled with a severed head
       as companion. The bond
       between you all

intensifies,
even as the flies
multiply around the sullied
cloth bag on the passenger seat.
This is not *grand guignol*
but a deeply personal
gaze into the moral

abyss, in which we find
ourselves now too,
reeling from the shovel-blow
that clatters you
into an open grave.
We're all in the dark
until you wake,

buried alive,
your mouth and eyes
clogged with dirt,
entangled, in your frantic
effort to escape, with the limp
body of the woman you love.
But how are we to ease

ourselves from the scene
where you look down
at one of your dead
assailants and pump
him with more bullets
and the gratuitous words:
because it feels so goddamned good.

The Killer Elite

The new west has none
of the poetry of old.
I can't pretend I'm not
at first disappointed.
Even San Francisco Bay
is painted gunmetal grey
… which is when I begin

        to get it, this cold-
        blooded, labyrinthine
        thriller about a sub-set
        of the CIA, hired assassins
        whose existence they deny
        while admitting that denial
        is their business. And yes,

we have to laugh at that—
and the way you steer
your story into satire:
a traffic cop handed
a ticking bomb
from beneath a getaway
taxi; a body turning up

      with luggage at the airport,
      a flasher there to distract
      the guards. And yet
      the heart of this is personal
      as ever: a character knee-
      capped by his partner, but
      refusing to accept

that his days are done.
We watch him (James Caan)
rebuild both body and career,
enduring ridicule
as a cripple—so cruel,
but filmed with aplomb,
the editing clinically sharp

          as any work of the elite
          on screen. And for this
          we sit through scenes
          that verge on the inept,
          those you may
          have simply failed to direct
          while snorting cocaine.

Soldiers Three

Ringo Starr and Harry Nilsson
are to join Keith Moon
in a boys' own remake
of the 1950s Robert Newton
original (RN Keith's hero).
The drummer's claim,
live on TV, is that you

>are the director who'll run
>with this silliness. Not true—
>though you will soon
>stoop to a song by CW McCall.
>But yes, you, Keith
>and Graham Chapman
>were an embattled trio

on the trail of delusion.
Three Serious Drinkers
providing proof
that an alcohol habit
was insufficient credit
for a productive team
of creative thinkers.

Python's *Salad Days* spoof
of your trademark style
had made you laugh,
their oh-so-British game
of tennis ending with
a racquet in the stomach
of a Merchant Ivory girl

and a flying piano
keyboard slicing through
some random
bystander's neck.
Later, Chapman had a go
at saving your Julian Lennon
documentary, to no avail.

As for his *Yellowbeard*—all
that yo-ho-ho hokum,
with Moon to play him-
self as the pirate fool—
you rated it zero.
Better the low-budget hell-hole
of tackling World War II.

Cross of Iron

A German folk tune
accompanies a montage
of newsreel footage:
Hitlerjugend—young boys
setting out to be men.
Each moving image
freezes to a blood-red still,

> then resumes, monochrome
> until your actors begin
> to permeate what is seen.
> As the children's voices fade,
> *Directed by Sam Peckinpah*
> explodes from a shell
> in a gothic-scripted blaze

across the screen.
For a moment I read it
as German, Beckenbach,
your family's original name.
We're near the end of the war
in this mud-drenched hell
of ruptured bodies

suspended in mid-fall …
but there, filling the frame
of what I most recall
is a Russian boy prisoner
throwing his harmonica
to Corporal Steiner,
who releases him by error

into the line of fire.
When Steiner's platoon—
stranded—heads back
towards its fate,
one young soldier hops
and steps in ungainly leaps,
trying to avoid

the dappled sunlight
on the forest floor.
He's a small boy again,
lost in a favourite game—
a no man's land of his own—
seeking to be honoured
with childlike luck.

Post-production

… has more than a touch
of the post-modern.
You're still in full flow
when they tell you to stop:
the money has run out.
The actors must improvise
a final scene.

    The Prussian captain
    fumbles with his gun,
    unable to reload,
    his helmet falling off.
    He and Steiner laugh
    at the shambolic closure,
    the Russian boy soldier—

back from the dead—
shaking his head
as his gun too jams.
He's complicit in this farce
that becomes a critique
of how war will never cease;
incompletion

turned into an art.
Next day, in your shell-
shocked, drugged delusion,
further sequences begin
to crystallize in your mind,
but the money-men
repeat: it's a wrap.

You'll have to make
do with the freeze-
framed laughter, an end
that loops back to the start—
a chilling reprise
of the children's bright
kindergarten rhymes.

You reload the screen
with a merciless slideshow,
the credits intercut
with civilian victims,
hard to watch.
And even this carousel
concludes where it began.

Convoy

Along for the ride,
we're quick to spot you
as part of the film crew
manoeuvring alongside
the trucks to get an interview.
*What's the purpose
of the convoy?*

       asks the clean-cut guy
       with the mic,
       sent by the state governor.
       To keep moving
       replies the Rubber Duck.
       Next they try their luck
       with the Old Iguana

(your own preferred nick-
name) in the truck
behind: *Where
were you born, Sir?*
His baffling answer
begins *Originally?*—
and it finally

    dawns on me
    this is a trail of smoke
    and mirrors, the Duck's
    inscrutable blue eyes
    behind silvered shades
    steering a course
    for his own demise

and resurrection. A hail
of bullets from Dirty Lyle
will blow his truck's
incendiary cargo
to hell,
even while
he lives to tell the tale.

    What we expect less
    is that somehow you too
    will survive this fiasco—
    the producer's tirades—
    and without even proving
    your worth, stroll away
    from your best payday.

Montana, 1978

The Greyhound bus
could take us only so far.
We sat at the roadside
drinking Colt 45s.
An old rocker pulled up
in an open-topped jeep
and offered us a ride.

> Keith Moon had just died,
> he said, as if that justified
> his spontaneous pilgrimage
> to Alaska, his luggage
> a single spade.
> We knew, even as we shook
> our heads, that a fork

in the road of our lives
had vanished for good.
Or, of course, bad.
We downed our beers,
hauled our make-
shift homes to our backs
and set out on foot.

None of this is of note
except for the fact that,
to reach Yellowstone
from Livingston,
we had to hitch the route
you used to take
from the Murray

to your mountain retreat
in Six Mile Creek,
and so it now strikes
me that on another day
it could have been you
who helped us on our way.
As night fell in the park

    we made a fire,
    rustled up simple food
    and to follow—a few
    far-fetched yarns to ward
    off our growing fears
    of a first, freezing night
    in the company of bears.

Cabin Fever

Your mountain paradise
is still a building site
in the wilderness.
Driving there, you pass
a couple of long-haired
backpackers, thumbs
outstretched. Last time

      you hosted any students
      it ended up in a fight
      and a lawsuit, so fuck 'em.
      Your children have fared
      little better in those moments
      when the bleak hollow
      of this troubled space

fomented a storm.
There's no electricity, no
plumbing. You sleep
with a loaded shotgun
pointed at your own face.
Unspeakable is the term
your daughter Sharon

resorts to. This is not
the Nation of Green, but
its terrible shadow, a place
where *Castaway* once more
takes a grip on your soul.
It's both your *ace in the hole*
and the stuff to fuel

your darkest dreams.
Even as you strike a deal
to finally get it made—
perhaps with Per Oscarsson,
LQ Jones or Peter O'Toole—
it spools uselessly in your head.
You raise a glass right here,

       where a friend has installed
       a beautifully crafted bar,
       and thrust the blade
       of your hunting knife deep
       into its timber,
       as if it's some desperate
       argument you might've nailed.

PART II

Castaway

Dawn, and from the moment
        you open your eyes, you know
                something's wrong with the light,
                      like the smell of bad meat.
                              A sickly orange glow leaks

    from the outside world
        as if from an apocalypse.

Something's wrong, too, with the geometry
    of the cabin. A delimited space
        you've always been able to gauge
            as you cross it in the dark
                now stretches way beyond

    plausible misjudgement,
        beyond the scope of your vision,

poor as that is, today, like yesterday,
    and so often, while body and mind
        drag themselves from the fog
            of last night's alcohol, or cocaine.
                You reach for the hair of the dog

    but it's not there in this strange scene
        you must have forgotten you planned to shoot.

As daylight grows, detail
    begins to materialize,
        the lines of a preparatory
            drawing, colour gradually filling in
                until what you behold—

    bewildered—is one floor
        of a vast department store:

a receding grid
              of innumerable aisles
                          and long counters of merchandise,
                                     some with locked glass cases for more
                                                 valuable or restricted goods.

              Silence thrums inside your head
                          as you stare at the deserted plenty, then

slowly—aware of your every footfall—
              walk towards the automatic doors
              which don't move.   Across
                          the inaccessible foyer is a screen
                                     of further security grilles,

              trapping you in this luxurious jail. You look
                          back with a new sense of your predicament.

There's an open steel cube
              of an elevator; empty, inert.
                          Every button you jab
                                     does nothing but raise
                                                 your frustration and incubating fear.

              Trying to stay calm, you walk
                          to the adjacent doors which open

onto stairs leading up …
              … and down, into darkness …
                          You lift your gaze to where
                                     light filters in and accentuates
                                                 the angular flights of steps and steel

              railings into a visual abstraction.
                          You read the key to the floors:

toys, games, maternity goods, baby supplies;
    cosmetics, perfumes, toiletries;
        rugs, carpets, curtains, cushions;
            men's and women's clothing, shoes;
                furniture …

    You memorize
        those floors that might be useful:

groceries, wine and spirits;
    kitchenware, tableware … ;
        sporting and camping equipment, guns;
            and now you have to choose
                as you bound up the steps …

    You need to eat. A tin of sardines
        comes with its own key, which you're quick

to twist—to reveal
    the tightly packed oily fish
        inside. You can't help your fingers from
            delving right in, scooping
                the pungent protein

    into your mouth
        with the clumsy urgency of a child.

But even while you smack
    your lips, something intrudes
        on your slightly smug repast,
            almost inaudible at first,
                but then again, the same, dull,

    intermittent thud
        that could be anything, but which you now hear

as a primordial threat
>   making you run
>   >   for the stairwell,
>   >   >   trying to remember
>   >   >   >   the floor, the number

>   on which your very existence
>   >   suddenly depends—

sporting and camping equipment
>   and surely ... but you've taken
>   >   the wrong exit and walk out
>   >   >   into *tableware and glass*.
>   >   >   >   Your eyes swivel from pots and pans

>   to crystal decanters, elegant candlesticks—
>   >   the wherewithal for a ghostly banquet.

You find the blocks of knives
>   and instinctively select
>   >   the largest and most dangerous
>   >   >   from the carefully graded display.
>   >   >   >   You admire it, before

>   tucking it inside the strap
>   >   of your belt, comforted.

And now you can roam
>   with new freedom
>   >   past lingerie-clad mannequins,
>   >   >   pausing to sample perfumes
>   >   >   >   that speak to you of lovers and wives

>   before you reach a maze of beds
>   >   on which your troubled reveries become a drowse.

* * *

You don't know how long
    you've been sleeping when
        a growling noise breaks
            into your dreams ...
                You're on your feet in a flash,

    scanning your surrounds
        for a wolf, a beast, any source

of the guttural sound
    which raises the hairs on your neck.
        Then you see it, the escalator grinding
            into action, even as the overhead lights
                flicker on, off, on; off.

    But the escalator keeps going,
        and you're drawn towards it, an iron pin

in some magnetic field.
        You step on and glide forward
              without moving a muscle, and there,
                      facing you at the top,
                              is a grand arsenal of firearms.

        For a moment you're stumped
              by the heavy-duty locks ... yet recklessly ram

your left elbow
        through the protective glass—howl
              with pain as blood seeps
                      through your lacerated shirt ...
                      but nestled in the mess

        of bloody glass fragments
              is everything you might need.

You grab a rifle, and cram
        ammunition into every pocket.
              Adding flashlights and batteries
                      to your haul, you soon outpace
                            the moving stairs, heading down again

        to *furniture*, to build yourself a hideout
              from any perils and dangers of the night.

You prop your gun against a cupboard
        and push the adjacent desk
              across to the wall by the restrooms.
                    Back for another, you're thrown
                    to find your weapon

        ... no longer there ... ... In panic, you spin
            around to see a multitude

of cupboards, wardrobes, mirrors,
    desks—so many that you keep
        spinning until, giddy, you adjust
            and finally locate
                your gun precisely where it was.

    You resume your task,
        the rifle at your side.

It's late afternoon,
    the meagre light almost gone,
        as you crawl onto the mattress
            within your improvised fortress
                and hold your gun close;

    darkness the enemy now
        as your flashlights start to fade

★ ★ ★

The soft growl
        starts up and you're pulled
                once more onto the treadmill
                        of anxiety—including the banal
                                but pressing need for the toilet ...

It's close to hand but the flush
        fails to work. And there's no water from the faucet.

Armed and hungry, you take
        the rumbling escalator down
                to *groceries*, and as you make
                        your silent arrival
                              see, some twenty yards away,

        with its strange, slumped
                back to you, a long-haired figure, engrossed

in eating from a can.
        You freeze.
                Slowly, you raise your rifle
                        to your shoulder, but the figure slips
                              sideways into another aisle.

        You wait, listening for footsteps,
                but there's only that monotonous grind.

Edging forward, half-
        crouched, peering over
            and between
                    the laden shelves of food,
                        you finally catch sight

        of a disappearing shadow,
                and now you're on the trail

of … you don't know what,
    except that it's a threat
        to your attempt at being lord
            and master of all you survey,
                and when the dark shape

    looms again in the distance
        you take aim with greater speed—

fire and reel
    from the sharp kickback
        on your shoulderbone,
            even as you realize
                the figure is gone

    from where bottles
        now lie smashed and weeping.

You creep forward
    to the wreckage.
        Glass. White wine.
            And there, within the puddles,
                a small drop of red

    from which you can be sure
        your quarry has been hurt.

There's a trail
    of further spots of blood,
        leading to the stairs …
            but it goes cold.
                Faltering, blank, you decide

    on down, no longer mindful
        of labelled floors but simply following

your every hunch,
    every scuff of dust on a step,
        and finally pushing through doors
            to the utterly unexpected—
                a sight that makes you gasp ...

    Christmas, as of old;
        the ephemeral magic intact ...

a magisterial tree
    and its acolytes—strung
        with gold-white pinecone bulbs and
            tinsel winding around each branch,
                a glint in every bauble and silver star.

    You wander through
        the glittering forest, losing yourself

in memories,
    your children standing
        right there to greet
            you, smiling, before they show
                first doubt, then growing alarm

    at how you might react.
        The faintest sound seems to come

from behind you. You snap
    out of your trance and turn
        to stare as if
            directly into camera, or
                at someone shadowing

    your every move. You see
        no-one, but your gaze

slowly falls
> to where your own
>> blood-smudged footprints
>>> have gone unseen. You wheel
>>>> around to see more drops

> of blood leading through the forest
>> that's now a thicket of your fears.

In the eerie silence,
> you follow the path
>> of red spots through the trees
>>> like breadcrumbs or stones
>>>> in a childhood storybook,

> the tree lights failing one
>> by one, until you are enveloped in gloom.

It feels like fate
> as you trudge to the far
>> corner of the room,
>>> guided only by the whine
>>>> of something—no, a *person*

> in distress. A dark, huddled form
>> quivers as it groans. You grasp

the whimpering creature
> from behind, almost like a lover,
>> slip the kitchen knife
>>> from your belt and draw
>>>> its factory-sharp blade

> across the invisible throat,
>> cruel to be kind, perhaps, or the reverse …

You can feel the hot
> blood coating your fingers as you hold
>> the crumpling body pulling you in tandem
>>> to the floor—can feel, too,
>>>> how it is to have that thing we call life

  drain away.
> And now it's death you embrace,

>>> hauling the full weight
>>>> of what you have lost
>>> to face you—the fright
>>>> of your own eyes, clear
>> as in a mirror,
>>>> heart
>> clamped tight in your chest.

PART III

The Emergency Room

A convention of nurses
just happens to be on hand
when you're found
close to death's door.
It's down to a Dr Noteboom
to wrangle with your heart
in the emergency room.

    A temporary pacemaker
    is being replaced
    with a permanent one
    when the wires get crossed.
    All you see is your lost
    heartbeat on screen,
    and so begins the tantrum.

What you want is a friend
who'll bring you drugs.
Even in your hotel
there are more quaaludes
than here in hospital.
JS will only give you hugs.
When released,

>you ignore all medical
>advice and head straight
>to the hotel bar.
>You order a Ramos Fizz—
>a huge tumbler of gin
>with egg-white—and smile
>as you raise it

to your lips. Friends watch
as you despatch
it in a couple of swigs,
then suddenly clutch
your chest, and in painful
slow motion fall
backwards off your stool

>to the barroom floor.
>Deathly silence concludes
>with your inevitable grin,
>though your friends take a
>while to follow suit.
>No vacancy quite yet
>within the Nation of Green.

Montana, 1979

Nearby, Cimino,
Hollywood's new hotshot,
is filming *Heaven's Gate*
with an Oscar-laden ego,
an attitude so profligate
he's taking the studio
to the brink.

>You agree to meet
>at the Outlaw Inn
>where people crowd
>to see the pair of you
>deep in conversation.
>He wants to know
>if you, in your heyday,

used this much ammo.
And will you work with him?
For a while you run
with the adulation,
no longer the frail man
with a pacemaker stead-
y-ing his wayward heart.

You could maybe do it—
directing second unit,
you're not proud—
but you see the money
bleeding from the picture,
and can see, too,
how such indulgence

will limit your chance
of ever having freedom
to make film your own way.
As lunch drags on
you feel the stricture
like a noose,
retreat

        to your hotel hideout,
        pour yourself a drink,
        sit restlessly alone
        and fire round
        after round at imagined
        intruders, or any
        other demons on the loose.

Latigo Productions

Named after the canyon
where your sister once lived,
business now consists
mainly of lawsuits
piling up in these rooms
of your hotel fortress.
The decor is ... curious.

> There's the ochre couch
> on which the *Straw Dogs* rape
> took place—you want
> its provenance to be known,
> should anyone hope
> to be made comfortable.
> Six Picassos look on

from the walls
beside posters and stills
from your films—a shrine
complete with the Remington
that now gets little use
as you handwrite poems
for Marcy, your new wife:

*Loneliness is a thin line
My gift
But not for you
For me and mine.*
The stormy marriage lasts
a mere month and a half
before it's annulled.

Whenever you do
pull on your cowboy boots
and venture grouch-
like into the outside world,
you carry a soft
toy monkey—consultant
on all important deals

      and even any mundane
      questions; accomplice
      and strange companion,
      loyal as any you've loved.
      He keeps a poker face,
      a demeanour inscrutable
      as your own.

The Osterman Weekend

Hopper, Lancaster, Hurt …
they all sign up for this
final chance to work
with a legend. You need
to justify their trust—
deliver the film on time
and within budget.

    It's not a great book
    or adaptation, but there's
    something at the core
    that you could turn
    to good effect—if allowed.
    Sober, you manage
    to resist a full-scale war

with the young-gun
cheapskates in search
of their own fame.
Instead, you take
a more subtle approach,
encouraging your cast
to improvise their lines

while you fill the big screen
with small ones
and relentlessly switch
from one surveillance
to another, until we doubt
what we see. Crossbows
on the pool-house wall

look like a crude
Straw Dogs reference;
when the family dog goes
missing, we fear the worst,
but a quick schlock reveal
of the animal's head
in an opened fridge

proves to be a joke—
mainly on us.
*The truth is just a lie that
hasn't been found out,*
says Bernie Osterman.
And every prescient message
here poses as deceit.

Too Late for Goodbyes

On the drive to the location
you throw a toddler's fit—
and cream of broccoli soup
into the producer's lap.
When he passes the test
with good humour, you
relax and get a grip

      on the challenge ahead—
      music videos for the up-
      and-coming Julian Lennon,
      risking fame in the wake
      of his father's blood.
      You're a world apart
      from the MTV generation

but want to embrace it
and prove you're not
redundant, an old west relic.
BearTracks studio, New York,
is cavernous, dark
as your Montana hideout.
You think on your feet

and open a backlit
doorway, in which an angelic
imp-like lookalike will strike
poses—comic, yet sad—
to pull Julian's attention,
and suddenly, father and son
are there in bittersweet

reunion, your cameras
calmly looking on.
For the second song, 'Valotte',
the metaphorical mirrors
within the lyric
are manifest on set.
You capture Julian

leaving his piano, the artist
walking away from his art
to better appreciate
what he hears.
In the control room, a man
supposedly at work stares out
as if he's simply enjoying it.

On the Rocks

When you fail to make
any progress, you recruit
your writing partner of old,
Jim Silke, to help you work
on the new script. I say
'new', but JS is quick
to recognize the lead

>characters as Blassingame
>and Smith—now called
>(with tongue firmly in cheek)
>Sam and Silk. You've pulled
>him in whether he likes it
>or not. And since the task
>is (oh god) *writing,* your ploy

is to delay, with a trip
to the shops at Point Dume.
How easily the two of you slip
back into the same
routine: you get the meat,
JS the coffee, the bread
and peanut butter, before

      the inevitable argument
      over flavours of ice cream.
      You're plain furious
      that he always chooses
      vanilla, as if it's a sign
      that his creative input
      will be similarly bland.

But you trust him
like no other—and
the procrastinating ritual
is one whereby you hope
to form some mutual
understanding of what
lies ahead; to dare to ask

      the simple question:
      Can anything be done?
      Or is this the moment
      you've known would come:
      The End. No more
      haggling over every scene,
      every word.

The Ones That Got Away

So many projects lie
abandoned: *The Texans*,
Michener's *Caravans*,
The Insurance Company,
The Monkey Wrench Gang.
Writing for Walt Disney
you failed to include

> enough children or dogs.
> With some you lost control:
> Brando's *One-Eyed Jacks*,
> *The Cincinnati Kid*,
> *Villa Rides* and *The Dice of God*.
> Some you turned down:
> *Superman, King Kong*...

Some didn't come your way:
*Deliverance, Jeremiah Johnson,
Emperor of the North Pole,
The Glass Menagerie, Play
It As It Lays* by Joan Didion
and other books
you had your eye on:

*Something Wicked
This Way Comes, First Blood,
Sometimes a Great Notion;*
several by your old pal,
Max Evans: *One-Eyed Sky,
The Great Wedding*—
and above all others

The Hi-Lo Country,
which would eventually fall
to Stephen Frears.
The list goes on, with rumour
in the mix (*Duck You Sucker*)
or where some fucker
was trying to bankroll

a project in your name: *King
of Nothing; The Last Running.*
So many that might have been;
Castaway perhaps still
waiting for a saviour.
Consider though the marvel
that any were made at all.

Begonia

Wives got away too,
for better or for worse,
victims but survivors
of your relentless rage—
and irrepressible fear
that you would forever
be the one betrayed.

> Three times you married
> Begonia Palacios,
> the Mexican actress
> who personified
> your adopted country—and
> the obsessive baggage
> that went with it.

Twice divorced,
many more times she ran
away, or you forced
her out—marriage
as tough a battleground
as any picture you made.
She alone could match

      your theatrical
      and impetuous behaviour,
      while taking all too much
      on the chin
      when it got dirty.
      Marie, Joie, Marcy, lovers
      aplenty, but it was Begonia

who would stop you
from being even lonelier
than you were.
She's there at the end,
inconsolable, hysterical.
Samuel es muy fuerte …
Surely you'd pull through.

      Her ashes will be thrown
      off shore at Malibu Beach,
      like yours. Her daughter,
      the long suffering Lupita,
      will revisit your log cabin
      to make a film of her own:
      Peckinpah Suite.

Solomon's Island

I track the place down
on the Cornish coast,
the house that was cast
as the Sumners' farm.
It's all much the same,
although the old garage
is now solar panelled.

> I think of your quote
> from the Tao Te Ching:
> *Heaven and earth are ruthless*
> *and treat the myriad people*
> *as straw dogs. The sage*
> *is ruthless and treats*
> *the people as straw dogs.*

Solomon: the archetypal
sage. But is it wisdom
or folly to holiday here alone
with no wifi, TV,
not even a landline
as there is in the film
for the call that ignites

the locals' rage
and the ensuing siege?
I can't, as I had planned,
watch your Cornish western
on location. Instead,
I let scenes from this
and that re-

run inside my head—
a bewildering montage
with Dundee reaching
for his sword; a child
in a coffin; Steve Judd
falling beyond the frame
of an autumnal world ...

*I didn't expect it
to be so sad*,
my daughter had said
as we came to the end.
I throw more logs
into the inglenooked stove;
feel savaged by love.

Paradise Cove

Everybody dies.
We're all so bloody good
at ignoring the obvious.
But you—you'd been
promising it for so many years
that the shock was hard
to explain. The word

      spread from one phone
      call to another—a whirl-
      wind of gathering dismay
      that the hurricane-
      level influence
      on so many Hollywood
      and other lives

had subsided, once
and for all. In the days
to come, there'd be news
for the rest of us, those
who knew the brilliance
of your work on film
without the body blows

of first-hand experience
in its making—no claim
to anything more than
sadness. I am not
there as family gather
on the shore, not there
under dark morning skies

as your son and brother-
in-law row a small boat
out to sea, open the urn
and cast handfuls
of your ashes on the waves,
followed by flower petals,
and finally, in her absence,

        one long-stemmed yellow rose
        after another, from Joie,
        last of your true wives.
        There'll be a time to share
        what here is precious
        and properly private;
        to let a wider grief unfurl.

Sunset Boulevard

A cruel week later
a cast of veterans assembles
at the Directors Guild Theater
for a public farewell.
They're not in great shape
but can still joke: *If we knew
we would live this long*

> *we'd have taken better care
> of ourselves.* It's pure
> Peckinpah—starts late,
> and no one has a clue
> what the hell is going on.
> They'd all once sworn
> never to work for you again,

but here they are, loyal
to the bitter beyond.
Each distinguished rogue
has a story, a poem, or song.
And he, who as Hogue
was eulogized onscreen,
offers you Shakespeare

in fitting return.
Our revels now are ended.
These our actors, as I
foretold you, were all
spirits and are melted
into air, into thin air…
And now I too can be there

without any corporeal
pretence—part
of a virtual brotherhood
(if not the Nation of Green),
all of us insubstantial
without your command.
For one last time we lean

in as if we might glean
your habitual mumbles
within Jason's desert-dry
speech. *We are such stuff*
as dreams are made
on, and our little life
is rounded with a sleep.

CODA

The Racquet Club

Every day, you post
photos of yourself at work
with friends on facebook.
I scroll through notifications:
*Sam Peckinpah responded
to one of your comments.*
You, but not you; an avatar

> curating our ongoing need
> to discuss and pay tribute
> to your genius. Each gem
> from the private collections
> of your closest clan
> enriches our shared sense
> of archival wealth.

Recent talk is of the heist
whereby your personal cut
of *Pat Garrett and Billy the Kid*
was retrieved from MGM,
a second break-in required
when the burglars found
it was an interlock

    print with the sound
    on separate reels. Paranoid,
    you re-labelled them
    The Racquet Club.
    Half a century later,
    restoration complete,
    your online hub

is buzzing with opinion.
For every diehard fan
of Dylan's 'Knock-knock-
knockin' on heaven's door'
there's another for whom
it's an intrusive whine.
But while this suite

    of rooms is mine
    I'll side with your own
    ambivalence—take
    the quarrel itself as a sign
    that the poetry and passion
    of your uproarious art
    are in rude health.

Afterword

Sam Peckinpah, writer and director, was born in Fresno, California, in 1925, 100 years before this book's publication. A notoriously 'difficult' character, he developed a style of film-making that was hugely influential though also highly controversial. The best of his work is still revered, and even those projects on which he lost control—either with producers or his own worst self to blame—are finding new critical acclaim after restoration.

Peckinpah bought his plot of land in Montana from Warren Oates in 1977. It was very much a 'project', rather than a dream fulfilled, and he spent most of his Montana years, especially after his heart attack, at the Murray Hotel in Livingston, where his suite of rooms has since been named in his memory.

I passed through Livingston in 1978 with 'Nosh', my travelling companion from school. I credit our teachers, Steve Room and David Dunford, for introducing us to Peckinpah's films.

Although Peckinpah, with his writing partner Jim Silke, made numerous attempts to adapt James Gould Cozzens' novella *Castaway*, their ambition to bring it to the screen was never realized. In 2018, however, it was announced that Milos Antic and Peckinpah's close friend and associate Katy Haber would be co-producing a version, but no further news has been forthcoming.

The phrase 'like a man in a green suit walking in a forest' was Gordon Dawson's beautiful description of Jerry Fielding's original score for *The Getaway*, which was replaced by a score by Quincy Jones. Jones was magnanimous in enabling Fielding eventually to release his original soundtrack on CD. Fielding, whose scores for both *The Wild Bunch* and *Straw Dogs* were nominated for an Oscar, withdrew from scoring *Pat Garrett and Billy the Kid*, as he loathed the inclusion of Bob Dylan's song, 'Knockin' on Heaven's Door'. Peckinpah's personal cut of the film excludes the lyric, and is now available as part of a multi-disc release from Criterion.

Should anyone know why Peckinpah included the MUNDENS sign so prominently in a pivotal scene in *The Getaway*, I'd be most grateful for the information.

For what it's worth, the 42 poems of Parts I and III, with Prelude and Coda, are all written in the 'Munden' form of 42 half-rhyming lines, in six stanzas of seven lines each. Part II deviates: 42 *sections* of seven lines, also half-rhyming across the whole. What can I say: mavericks can also be formalists, and obsessive.

I trust there's not much else that needs explaining—at least, not if the reader were to (re)watch the films, which is one of the things I most hope for in publishing this book. For a detailed biography, I recommend *"If they move... Kill 'Em!": The Life and Times of Sam Peckinpah* by David Weddle.

Paul Munden

Sam Peckinpah at his cabin in Montana,
courtesy of the Sam Peckinpah Facebook page.

Acknowledgements

A number of the *Peckinpah Suite* poems have previously appeared in *Axon: Creative Explorations, Western Humanities Review,* and *Wild Court.*

A chapter exploring the process of the poems, '*Peckinpah Suite*: Revisiting the Films of Sam Peckinpah in Verse', is to appear in a forthcoming book from Routledge, *Ekphrastic Approaches in Twenty-First Century Poetry: Writing Out*, edited by Oz Hardwick and Amina Alyal.

Special thanks are due to Oliver Comins, whose close reading and editorial suggestions were enormously helpful; also, as ever, to Shane Strange, publisher, whose fearless and tireless commitment to poetry is now a decade strong.

About the Author

Paul Munden is a poet, editor and screenwriter living in North Yorkshire. His first paid work was as reader for Stanley Kubrick. He was director of the UK's National Association of Writers in Education for nearly 25 years, and more recently a Royal Literary Fund Fellow at the University of Leeds. He lived in Australia for several years, running Poetry on the Move, the festival initiated by the University of Canberra, to which he remains affiliated as an Adjunct Associate Professor. He has published six previous poetry collections, including *Amplitude* (Recent Work Press, 2022), and many chapbooks, most of which include at least one Peckinpah poem. He is also the author of *Unclassified: Nigel Kennedy in Chapters & Verse*, a study of the maverick violinist.

https://paulmunden.com

It bugged you for years—
forgetting the drone of flies
to be dubbed into the edit
of the Bunch's demise.
Already I feel the threat—
an omission of my own
never letting me alone.

www.ingramcontent.com/pod-product-compliance
Lightning Source LLC
Chambersburg PA
CBHW020541080526
44583CB00013B/941